CRUEL TIMES

A Victorian play

Kaye Umansky

For Ella – K.U.

ABOUT THE AUTHOR

Kaye Umansky is best known as the creator of Pongwiffy, the 'witch of dirty habits', whose hilarious antics feature in five books. She is a former teacher with special interests in drama and music, and has written many plays for performance.

CRUEL TIMES

A Victorian play

Kaye Umansky

Illustrated by Martin Ursell

HODDER
Wayland

an imprint of Hodder Children's Books

INTRODUCTION

The year is 1855, and Queen Victoria has been on the throne for 18 years. The British Army is fighting a war in the Crimea. The Prime Minister, Benjamin Disraeli, calls Britain "two nations". One nation consists of people living comfortable lives. The poor, who work for very low wages, often in appalling conditions, make up the other nation. The lives of these two groups of people are very different.

This play explores the lives of a wealthy family and their staff. Four of the scenes are set in various rooms in the house, and two are set in a market.

The play is intended for reading in class in a single session. There are 29 speaking parts: 12 for girls, 12 for boys and five for either boys or girls. If necessary, one or two of the smaller roles (e.g. the market costermongers) can be omitted. The play can, however, be read in groups of four or five, with some children taking more than one of the smaller roles. This can be arranged on a scene-by-scene basis; the characters who appear in each scene are listed at the beginning.

THE CAST *in order of appearance*

Name	Description	Role
Mrs. Fry	The cook	Large
Sissy	The scullery maid	Large
Alice	} Kitchen maids	Medium
Ellen		Medium
Mr. Davy	The butler	Small
Mrs. Garnett	The housekeeper	Medium
Henry	The footman	Small

Jack	The pantry boy	Small
Miss Twaite	The governess	Medium
Rose	⎫	Small
Mary	⎬ The Nash children	Small
Arthur	⎭	Small
George Nash	A wealthy banker	Medium
Emily Nash	His wife	Medium
Fruitmonger (Male or female)	⎫	Small
Lavender Seller (Female)		Small
Fishmonger (Male or female)		Small
Watercress Seller (Male or female)	⎬ Costermongers	Small
Match Seller (Male or female)		Small
Egg Seller (Male or female)		Small
Muffin Seller (Male)	⎭	Small
Crossing Sweeper (Male)		Small
Beggarwoman		Small
Gentleman		Small
Lady		Small
Freddy	⎫	Small
Robbo	⎬ Urchins	Small
Spinks	⎭	Small
Charles Dickens	A famous writer	Large

SCENE 1

(Mrs. Fry, Sissy, Alice, Ellen, Mr. Davy, Mrs. Garnett, Henry, Jack)

*A Victorian kitchen in a large town house. It is furnished with a big iron range, a dresser and a wooden table. A mop in a bucket stands to one side. **Mrs. Fry**, the cook, is making a pie.*

Mrs. Fry: *(Shouts)* Sissy! Where's that jar of damson jam I asked for?

Sissy: *(Off-stage)* I'm looking for it, mum.

Mrs. Fry: And less of the mums! I'm not your ma. It's Mrs. Fry. I've told you before.

Sissy: *(Off-stage)* Sorry, mum.

Mrs. Fry: *(To the audience)* I dunno. Scullery maids these days. Thick as a navvy's arm, most of 'em. *(Shouts)* Where's that jam?

*(Enter **Sissy**, the scullery maid. She is nervous and breathless. She has a jar in her hand. **Mrs. Fry** snatches it.)*

Mrs. Fry: And about time. You want to look lively, my girl. There's plenty more who'd jump at your job. *(Examines jar)* Oh, my eye! This ain't

jam, you silly girl. This is pickled onions.
Can't you read? *(She gives the jar back)*

Sissy: No, mum, sorry, mum. Never went to school,
mum. Stayed at home and helped Ma with the
sewin'. Please don't fire me, mum. *(To audience)*
I really need this job. I gets a shilling a week,
and me board and lodgings. With me gone, it's
one less mouth to feed. There's six of us in the
family and another one on the way.

*(Enter **Ellen** and **Alice**, the kitchen maids,
with trays of dirty dishes. **Alice** seems
rather miserable.)*

Mrs. Fry: Where have you two been?

Alice: Collecting the breakfast dishes from upstairs,
Mrs. Fry.

Ellen: Like you said.

Alice: *(To audience)* That's all us kitchen maids ever
do. Run up and down stairs all day with trays
and buckets of coal. *(Sighs)*

Ellen: And bloomin' great jugs of hot water.

Mrs. Fry: Well, take the crocks through to the scullery,
then. And fetch me a jar of damson jam. It's gone
seven o'clock. We need to get cracking with
luncheon soon. *(Exit **Ellen** and **Alice**)* Don't just
stand there, Sissy. Get them crocks washed, then
make a start on peeling the potatoes.

SCENE 1

*(Enter **Mr. Davy**, the butler. **Sissy** collides with him. The jar of pickled onions falls to the floor and breaks.)*

Mr. Davy: Watch where you're going, you clumsy girl! Just look at this mess!

Sissy: Oh, sir! I'm sorry ...

Mrs. Fry: Now see what you've done, butterfingers. The whole place reeks of vinegar! Clean it up! Sorry, Mr. Davy. I'm doing my best to train her up, but it's a losing battle. I'm telling you, my girl. Mess up again and you're out of a job.

Sissy: Oh, but mum ...

Mrs. Fry: Did you hear me? Clean it up! And for the last time, don't call me mum!

(Sissy begins to pick up the glass.)

Mr. Davy: The master has a guest for dinner tonight, Fry. Mrs. Garnett's on her way down to discuss the menu. If anyone wants me, I'm in the wine cellar. *(To audience)* It's not a bad job, being a butler. Fair wages – about forty pounds a year, plus tips. I see high life and low life, above and below stairs. And I get treated with respect. *(Waves a superior hand)* Carry on.

(Mr. Davy stalks out.)

Mrs. Fry: *(Sniffs)* Mr. Flippin' High and Mighty. *(Shouts)* Ellen! Alice!

(Ellen and Alice return.)

Mrs. Fry: There's another for dinner, as if I don't have enough to do. Ellen, finish this pie crust. Make sure your hands are clean. And Alice, get this floor mopped before Mrs. Garnett starts swanning around giving her orders. Where's that jam?

Alice: I think we're out of damson, Mrs. Fry. There's plenty of gooseberry …

Mrs. Fry: Of course there's damson! There's a jar on the top shelf – I put it there myself. I dunno, if you want something doing, do it yourself. Out of my way!

SCENE 1

(Mrs. Fry exits. Sissy wipes away a tear with her apron.)

Ellen: What's up with you, Sissy?

Sissy: I dropped the pickles. She's mad at me again.

Alice: She's just got a lot on her plate, that's all.
Like we all have. *(Sighs)*

Sissy: But what if she fires me? What'll I do? I won't get another job without references, and Ma's relying on me sending money home.

Ellen: Then you'll just have to be a good girl and keep your nose clean, won't you? Oops! Here she comes.

(Ellen and Alice jump to attention. Enter Mrs. Fry with a jar of jam.)

Mrs. Fry: You see? What did I tell you? Damson jam, marked plain as a pikestaff. Have you picked all the glass up, Sissy?

Sissy: Yes, mu – Mrs. Fry.

Mrs. Fry: Then get washing them dishes. Hurry up with that floor, Alice.

(Sissy scuttles out, narrowly avoiding bumping into Mrs. Garnett, the housekeeper, who is holding a piece of paper.)

Sissy: 'Scuse, me, mu – Mrs. Garnett.

(She bobs a curtsey and exits. Mrs. Fry bows stiffly.)

Mrs. Fry: Morning, Mrs. Garnett. Say good morning to the housekeeper, girls.

Ellen and Alice: *(Curtseying)* Morning, ma'am.

Mrs. Garnett: Hmm. *(Stares coldly round the kitchen)* What's that smell, Fry?

Mrs. Fry: Vinegar. Sissy dropped a jar of pickles. Did you want something, Mrs. Garnett?

Mrs. Garnett: Yes. The Master is expecting company this evening.

Mrs. Fry: So I heard.

Mrs. Garnett: I've consulted with the Mistress and drawn up a list. First course: calf's head soup and broiled mackerel. Followed by calf's liver and bacon. Then roast loin of veal, boiled fowl with white sauce and boiled knuckle of ham. Fourth course: apple custard, blancmange and lemon jelly, followed by fruit and ices.

Mrs. Fry: Not sure about the ices, ma'am. The ice chest's empty. Waiting for the man to deliver.

Mrs. Garnett: Well, see that he does. Madam is most anxious that this evening should go well. *(To audience)* I run a tight ship. It's my responsibility to keep the accounts, hire and fire the staff and organise the shopping. In short, I give the orders around here. *(Points sternly to the floor and beckons to **Alice**)* You've missed a bit.

SCENE 1

*(Enter **Sissy**, in a panic.)*

Sissy: Please, Mrs. Fry ...

Mrs. Fry: What now, Sissy? I'm talking to Mrs. Garnett.

Sissy: But the water's gone cold. I can't get the grease off the crocks.

Mrs. Fry: Oh, drat! Not again. Ellen! Stoke up the range! Do I have to think of everything myself?

*(Enter **Henry**, the footman.)*

Henry: Excuse me, Mrs. Fry, but Miss Twaite's complaining that no one's been up to clear away the breakfast dishes in the nursery. She can't start the children's lessons. *(To audience)* I'm the footman. Not as highly respected as the butler, but I'm working on it.

Mrs. Garnett: Tch, tch, tch. What's this? Dishes still in the nursery? They should have been cleared away long ago.

Mrs. Fry: *(Scolding)* Ellen! I thought you were doing the nursery!

Ellen: I did the morning room. I thought Alice was doing it.

Mrs. Garnett: Well, I suggest you get yourselves more organised in future. Organisation! That's what it's all about. *(Severely)* This won't do, Fry. It won't do at all.

Mrs. Fry: *(Tightly)* It won't happen again, Mrs. Garnett.

SCENE 1

Mrs. Garnett: I sincerely hope not. I'll leave the list with you.

*(**Mrs. Garnett** sweeps out.)*

Mrs. Fry: Now see, you daft girls! You've put her in one of her moods. She'll be on my back all day now. As if I haven't got enough to worry about. Whatever were you thinking of, Alice?

Alice: *(Bursts into tears)* Oooh-hoo!

Mrs. Fry: Oh, lawks! What's up now?

Ellen: She's crying because her brother Charlie's away fighting in the Crimea, and they haven't heard from him.

Mrs. Fry: Yes, well, we've all got our problems. You should be grateful you've got a good position and a roof over your head. Dry your eyes and get up there quick, before that snooty governess comes down complaining. Ellen, go and help her. Henry, see if you can get that boiler working properly, there's a good lad. It's playing up again. Sissy, get cracking on those potatoes, or you'll feel the back of my hand.

*(Exit **Sissy, Alice** and **Ellen**. Enter **Jack** the pantry boy with a box of cutlery.)*

Mrs. Fry: And where have you been, young Jack?

Jack: Blacking the boots. *(Shows his black hands to audience)* It's a rotten job, pantry boy, but someone has to do it. Better than working in a sweatshop, I know that.

Mrs. Fry: I'll put my boot you know where if you're late again. Run out and see if you can catch the ice man. We need ice for the chest.

Jack: Can't. Mr. Davy said I've got to polish the knives.

Mrs. Fry: Later! Go, or I'll polish your ears.

Henry: Coal scuttle's getting low.

Mrs. Fry: Well, fill it up, then.

Henry: Not my job to deal with coal. And Mr. Davy says I'm to help him fetch the wine up.

*(Exit **Henry**.)*

Mrs. Fry: Jack! Fetch in some more coal!

Jack: I thought you said I was to get the ice man.

Mrs. Fry: Coal. Fetch. Now!

*(**Mrs. Fry** raises her hand. **Jack** exits in a hurry. **Mrs. Fry** consults the list.)*

Mrs. Fry: Eggs! I need more eggs for the custard. And fresh mackerel, and watercress, for garnish. *(Shouts)* Sissy! Stop what you're doing and come here.

*(Enter **Sissy**, at a run.)*

Sissy: Yes, Mrs. Fry?

Mrs. Fry: I need you to run to the market. You're to get a dozen eggs, three fresh mackerel and a bunch of watercress. Can you remember that?

Sissy: I think so. I mean, yes.

Mrs. Fry: Here's the money. Take a basket. Mind you don't get short-changed. And get back here in double-quick time.

Sissy: I will.

Mrs. Fry: Well, go on, then! What are you waiting for? Eggs, fish, watercress. Mess it up this time, and I'm telling you, it'll be the last thing you do in this house. I mean it, mind.

*(Exit **Sissy**. **Mrs. Fry** claps her hand to her head.)*

Mrs. Fry: It'll be the death of me, working in this kitchen!

SCENE 2

(Miss Twaite, Rose, Mary, Arthur, Ellen, Alice)

In the nursery. **Miss Twaite**, *the governess, sits tapping her foot. The three children – * **Rose**, **Mary** *and* **Arthur** *– sit in silence, holding their slates.*

Miss Twaite: Rose, sit up straight. What have I told you about posture? And Arthur, stop fidgeting with your slate. *(To audience)* So you think this is an easy job? Well, it's not. Particularly if one actively dislikes small children. As I do.

Rose: *(To audience)* We don't like her much, either.

Mary: *(To audience)* She never lets us have any fun.

Arthur: *(To audience)* She's a rotten teacher, too. She makes us do baby work. I want to learn about exciting things. Like trains.

Mary: May we play with the rocking horse, Miss Twaite? Just while we're waiting?

Miss Twaite: You certainly may not. Mornings are for lessons, not playing. Sit still and wait. Where is that fool of a maid?

(Impatiently, **Miss Twaite** *rings a handbell.)*

Arthur: Can't we have our lessons in the garden? It's sunny outside.

Miss Twaite: No. And if you don't sit still, I shan't take you for a walk this afternoon, so be warned.

Arthur: But …

Rose: Sssh, Arthur. Don't argue.

Miss Twaite: *(Coldly)* Thank you, Rose. If I need your assistance, I shall tell you.

*(There is a tap at the door. Enter **Alice** and **Ellen**, with trays. **Alice** is dabbing her eyes with her apron.)*

Ellen: Excuse me, Miss Twaite. We've come for the breakfast things.

Miss Twaite: And about time. How am I supposed to teach surrounded by filthy crockery?

Ellen: Sorry, Miss. Alice isn't feeling too good …

Miss Twaite: Yes, yes. Just clear away and go. We're already ten minutes late starting.

*(**Alice** and **Ellen** load their trays. **Alice** is still snivelling.)*

Rose: *(Kindly)* What's the matter, Alice?

Mary: Why are you crying? Did you hurt yourself?

Miss Twaite: I'll thank you to keep quiet, young ladies. Speak when you're spoken to. Whatever is wrong with her, it's none of our concern.

(To the maids) Hurry up!

*(**Alice** and **Ellen** exit with the breakfast things.)*

Alice: *(Weeping)* I'm just so worried about Charlie ...

Ellen: Sssh. I know.

Miss Twaite: Right. Draw up your chairs, children, and we will begin. Put your slates down and sit on your hands. We will start by reminding ourselves of our ABC. Arthur. You start.
(She points)

Arthur: *(Sighing)* "A" is for "apple", so round and so red.

Mary: "B" is for "bonnet", on Baby's sweet head.

Rose: "C" is for "candle" – we love its warm glow.

Arthur: "D" is for something, but what, I don't know.

(All three children giggle.)

Miss Twaite: *(Sharply)* Was that supposed to be funny, Arthur?

Arthur: I'm sorry, Miss Twaite. It's just that we've said it a hundred times.

Miss Twaite: You will be sorry, when you spend this afternoon writing it out a hundred times while I take the girls for a walk in the park.

Rose: Oh, no, Miss Twaite …

Mary: He didn't mean to be rude. Did you, Arthur?

Miss Twaite: Then he should think before he speaks. Good children should be seen and not heard. I shall have words with your father about you, young man.

Rose: Please don't, Miss Twaite.

Mary: He was only being silly.

Miss Twaite: Enough! We've wasted enough time as it is. As Arthur knows his ABC so well, we will move on to our multiplication tables. Starting with the two times. Loudly and clearly, if you please.

Children: One times two is two, two times two are four, three times two are six, four times two are eight, five times two are ten …

SCENE 3

(Emily Nash, George Nash)

In the morning room. **George Nash***, a wealthy lawyer, is reading* The Times. **Emily Nash***, his wife, is arranging flowers.*

Emily: Anything of interest in the paper, dearest?

George: More deaths in the Crimea.

Emily: Oh, dear. Thank heaven for Miss Nightingale. At least she's bringing the poor boys as much comfort as she can. Do you know what they're calling her? "The Lady with the Lamp".

George: She'll need more than a lamp to get that lot sorted out.

Emily: But at least she's trying. That's something.

George: True. *(To audience)* The name's Nash. George Nash. Husband, father, successful lawyer and head of the household. You'll notice that I'm the one with the paper. On the whole, women aren't expected to have opinions about the world – although my good wife Emily takes an interest. Unlike many men of my acquaintance, I encourage it. Unless she disagrees with me, of course. *(Returns to paper)*

Emily: Any other news?

George: Two more suspected cases of cholera in the
slums. It's not surprising with all that festering
rubbish lying around. And there's to be a
public hanging of some wretched pauper at
Newgate Gaol.

Emily: Those poor people. What dreadful lives
they lead.

24

George: Yes. Doubtless we'll hear all about it this evening, when Charles arrives. Social reform is a major passion of his.

Emily: I must say, I shall be intrigued to meet Mr. Dickens. I much enjoy his serialised stories. How did you come to meet him, George?

George: He used to work as a law court reporter. He's just returned from a reading tour, apparently. I bumped into him at the club. There's an article here by him, complaining about the plight of child chimney-sweeps.

Emily: Well, good for him! It's about time someone did something.

George: Yes. *(Standing)* Well, this won't do. I'm calling into the office this morning. Then I shall probably spend a hour or two at the club. How do you plan to occupy your day, my dear?

Emily: Oh, I don't know. A little embroidery, maybe. And I shall practise the piano and maybe visit the Hawkins sisters. And I want to choose some lace for my new gown, and bundle up some clothes for the poor. But of course, I shall make sure that everything is running smoothly for tonight. *(To audience)* Running the household is one of the few responsibilities we wealthy women have. I suppose you could call it work, of a sort. Although Mrs. Garnett takes most of it off my hands.

George: Goodbye, my dear. I shall be home in good time. *(Exits, with the paper)*

Emily: *(Sighs)* Goodbye, George. *(To audience)* Is it just me, or is my life rather empty?

SCENE 4

(Costermongers: Fruitmonger, Lavender Seller, Fishmonger, Watercress Seller, Match Seller, Egg Seller, Muffin Seller; Beggarwoman, Lady, Crossing Sweeper, Gentleman, Urchins: Freddy, Robbo and Spinks; Sissy)

A busy marketplace. **Costermongers** *cry their wares. The* **Crossing Sweeper** *leans on a broom. An old* **Beggarwoman** *pleads for change. A well dressed* **Gentleman** *and* **Lady** *move around examining the wares.*

Fruitmonger: Apples! Apples! Rosy and red! An apple a day keeps the workhouse away! Apples an' pears, hup the stairs!

Lavender Seller: Buy my sweet lavender, penny a bunch! Lavender for the lady, sir? They say it keeps away the cholera!

Fishmonger: Fish! Fresh fish! Herrings and mackerel! Yarmouth bloaters, three for a penny!

Watercress Seller: Watercress! Fresh watercress! Ha'penny a bundle! Come and buy!

Match Seller: Box of matches to light yer cigar, sir? Only a farthing for twenty!

Egg Seller: New-laid eggs, eight a groat! Crack 'em and try 'em!

Muffin Seller: *(Ringing his bell)* Who'll buy a muffin? Muffins for tea!

Beggarwoman: *(Tugging at the **Lady**'s skirts)* Spare a coin for a poor old woman, sir. I ain't had a bite in three days.

Lady: Ugh! Get your filthy hands off me! Let's go, William. If there's one thing I can't abide, it's beggars. Take your hand out of your pocket. Do you want to encourage her?

SCENE 4

*(The **Crossing Sweeper** leaps in front of the **Gentleman** and the **Lady**.)*

Crossing Sweeper: 'Old yer 'orses, missus! I'll sweep a path across the street for yer! Don't want to get yer hem dirty, do yer?

*(He sweeps a path. The **Lady** stalks across. The **Gentleman** produces a coin.)*

Gentleman: Here, boy. Here's a farthing for you. Spend it wisely.

Lady: William! What did I just say?

Gentleman: Coming, my dear!

*(The **Lady** and the **Gentleman** exit. Enter **Sissy** with a basket. She moves around the stalls, buying eggs, fish and watercress. A gang of **Urchins** – **Freddy**, **Robbo** and **Spinks** – enter, jostling each other.)*

Freddy: Gerroff, Robbo! You lookin' for a punch on the nose?

Robbo: Oh, yeah? And who's gonna give it me?

Freddy: Me, if yer don't lay off.

Spinks: 'Ere! Freddy! Dare yer to nick an apple!

Robbo: Yeah, go on!

Freddy: Why not you?

Robbo: 'Cos Spinks dared you, not me.

Spinks: Course, if yer too scared …

Freddy: I ain't scared.

Robbo: Yes, you are. *(To audience)* He is.

Freddy: Oh, yeah? Watch me, then!

> *(He goes to the **Fruitmonger***'s *barrow, snatches an apple and runs off, followed by **Robbo** and **Spinks**.)*

Urchins: Ha, ha!

Fruitmonger: Oi! Come back 'ere, yer little varmint! I'll 'ave the law on yer! Bloomin' kids.

> *(**Sissy** has finished her shopping. She stops by the **Beggarwoman**, fishes in her pocket and produces a coin.)*

Sissy: Here. It's not much, but it's all I can afford.

Beggarwoman: Bless your kind heart, dearie.

Sissy: You're welcome.

> *(The **Urchins** are hiding round the corner, greedily sharing the apple. **Sissy** approaches.)*

Spinks: Give us another bite, Freddy.

Freddy: Wait yer turn. 'Oo nicked it, anyway?

Robbo: Oho! Look what's comin'!

Spinks: Hey, you! Girl! What yer got in the basket?

> *(They surround **Sissy**.)*

Sissy: None of your business.

Freddy: Yer got a right feast in 'ere! Too much for one.

Robbo: Yer needs us to 'elp yer out.

Spinks: Yeah, right.

*(He snatches the basket and runs out, laughing, followed by **Robbo** and **Freddy**.)*

Sissy: Stop! Give me my basket, you horrible boys ...

Urchins: *(Off-stage)* Ha, ha, ha!

(**Sissy** *runs back to the marketplace.)*

Sissy: Help, somebody! Those boys, they've stolen my basket!

Fruitmonger: Apples! Rosy and red!

Lavender Seller: Lavender, penny a bunch!

Fishmonger: Fish! Come and get yer fish!

Watercress Seller: Watercress! Fresh watercress!

Match Seller: Matches! A farthing for twenty!

Egg Seller: New-laid eggs, eight a groat!

Muffin Seller: *(Ringing his bell)* Muffins! Who'll buy a muffin?

Beggarwoman: Take pity on a poor old woman!

Sissy: Oooooh! That's torn it. Whatever shall I do? *(She bursts into tears.)*

SCENE 5

(Charles Dickens, Sissy)

An alleyway off the marketplace. **Sissy** *sits on a barrel, sobbing into her apron. A well dressed stranger walks past and notices her.* **Sissy** *doesn't know it yet, but this is* **Charles Dickens**.

Charles Dickens: Dear me! So many tears. Quite a river. May I ask what is the cause of all this distress?

Sissy: Ooo hooo!

Charles Dickens: Here. Allow me to offer you my handkerchief. I assure you it's quite clean.

Sissy: *(Sniffing)* Ma says I'm not to take things from strangers.

Charles Dickens: My dear young lady, it's only a handkerchief. I mean you no harm. Come, now. Take it. Dry your eyes.

(He sits next to her, on another barrel. Hesitantly, **Sissy** *takes the handkerchief and blows her nose.)*

Sissy: Thank you.

Charles Dickens: What's your name, child?

Sissy: Sissy, sir.

Charles Dickens: So why all the tears, young Sissy?
It's a fine, sunny day. No fog, for once.
You should be all smiles. Are you hurt?
Has someone been beating you?

Sissy: No, sir.

Charles Dickens: What, then? You can tell me.
A problem shared is a problem aired, eh?

Sissy: Oh, sir! I'm in that much trouble! Our cook sent
me to buy some things from the market because
there's a special guest coming tonight, and some
boys stole my basket, and I've spent all the
money, and now I daren't go back and tell
her 'cos ...

Charles Dickens: Wait, wait. Slow down. Your basket has been stolen, you say?

Sissy: Yes. I couldn't help it, they surrounded me and ...

Charles Dickens: What was in it?

Sissy: The mackerel for tonight's dinner, and some watercress, and some eggs. Oh, whatever shall I do? The cook'll tell Mrs. Garnett, and she'll tell Mrs. Nash, and I'll lose my job!

Charles Dickens: Mrs. Nash?

Sissy: Yes. She's the lady of the house.

Charles Dickens: Mrs. George Nash?

Sissy: Yes. Do you know of her, sir?

Charles Dickens: I ... I've met her husband. So you are the cook's trusty assistant, eh?

Sissy: Oh, no! I'm just the scullery maid. It's my first job in service. Ma was so proud when I got taken on. And now I've gone and mucked it up.

Charles Dickens: You like your job?

Sissy: Well ... like's not the word. I don't get to sit down much, and the hours are long. Five in the morning 'til gone ten at night. But I get food and board, and seven pound a year. And now there won't be no more wages to send home, an' Ma's got all the little ones to feed ...

SCENE 5

Charles Dickens: What does your mother do, child?

Sissy: She's a shirt maker. But her eyes are going, and she can't earn enough to feed us all.

Charles Dickens: And your father?

Sissy: Dead and gone, sir, may he rest in peace. Happened last year. Accident in the iron foundry.

Charles Dickens: Ah, me. We live in cruel times. It's a hard world, Sissy.

Sissy: It is that, sir.

*(**Dickens** pauses, and then takes a coin from his pocket and holds it out.)*

Charles Dickens: But things can only get better, eh? A spot of sunshine in the gloom. Here. For you.

Sissy: *(Shocked)* A sovereign! I can't take this.

Charles Dickens: Nonsense! I insist. Buy some more fish and eggs, or whatever it is you need.

(He presses the coin into her hand.)

Sissy: But a whole sovereign! I don't need anything like this much …

Charles Dickens: So the rest is yours! Buy yourself a pretty bonnet, or some fresh fruit for your poor mother. Spend it as you will.

Sissy: But why, sir? Why are you doing this for me?

Charles Dickens: There is too much pain and hardship in life, young Sissy. Kindness is in short order. Sometimes I look around me and despair. But I do what I can.

Sissy: Oh, sir! How can I thank you?

Charles Dickens: Just make sure the mackerel is fresh. I'm rather fond of mackerel. Will it be broiled, do you think?

Sissy: *(Puzzled)* I think so.

Charles Dickens: Excellent, excellent. And now I must be on my way.

Sissy: What is your name, sir? If you don't mind my asking?

Charles Dickens: Dickens. Charles Dickens.

Sissy: What – the gentleman who writes them penny dreadful stories?

Charles Dickens: *(Chuckles)* That's me. Take care of yourself, my dear. Maybe we'll meet again, eh?

(He tips his hat and exits.)

Sissy: Sir! Mr. Dickens! You've forgotten your hanky ... A whole sovereign! This is my lucky day!

SCENE 6

(Mr. Davy, Charles Dickens, Emily Nash, Rose, George Nash, Miss Twaite, Mary, Arthur, Alice, Ellen, Henry)

In the dining room. It is evening. **George** *and* **Emily Nash** *and* **Charles Dickens** *sit at a groaning table. They are served by* **Alice** *and* **Ellen.** **Mr. Davy** *pours wine.* **Henry** *stands in the background, ready to assist.*

Mr. Davy: More wine, sir?

Charles Dickens: Thank you, I will.

Emily: Is the mackerel to your liking, Mr. Dickens?

Charles Dickens: Excellent, Mrs. Nash. My compliments to your cook.

(Enter **Miss Twaite**, *accompanied by* **Rose**, **Mary** *and* **Arthur**.*)*

Emily: Ah, children. Have you come to say goodnight?

Rose: Yes, Mother.

George: Have they behaved themselves today, Miss Twaite?

Miss Twaite: *(Stiffly)* I'd be lying if I said they've been angels, sir.

Emily: Oh, dear.

Charles Dickens: But then, what children are, eh? They look quite charming to me.

Emily: This is Mr. Dickens, children. The famous writer.

Rose and Mary: *(Bobbing)* How do you do, sir?

Arthur: I'm going to write a story when I'm bigger. A horror story, about a cruel old governess who gets eaten by rats!

Miss Twaite: Well, really!

George: That's enough, Arthur. Off to bed with you, now.

Emily: Goodnight, darlings. Sleep well.

Children: Goodnight, Mother. Goodnight, Father. Goodnight, Mr. Dickens.

*(They are hustled out by a furious **Miss Twaite**.)*

Emily: I really think we must look around for another governess, George. They don't seem to be learning a thing. And Arthur's becoming quite naughty.

Alice: Are you ready for the next course, ma'am?

Emily: Yes, thank you, Alice. You're looking rather more cheerful today.

Ellen: She's heard from Charlie, ma'am.

Emily: Oh, Alice! Really?

Alice: Yes, ma'am. The letter arrived today. He's been wounded in the leg, but at least he's alive. And they're sending him home!

Emily: Oh, I'm so glad! Do you hear that, George? Alice's brother is coming home.

George: Well, that is excellent news indeed.

*(**Alice**, **Ellen** and **Henry** clear the table and exit.)*

Emily: Mr. Dickens, I read your piece in the paper today. I must say I was quite shocked.

Charles Dickens: Good. That was my intention. And do call me Charles.

George: My wife is very interested in the plight of the poor, Charles. She has a tender heart.

Emily: It quite breaks me up to see how some people live. Particularly the children. Is there nothing that can be done?

Charles Dickens: Oh, yes. We mustn't give in to despair, Mrs. Nash. Change will come, slowly but surely. We just need to open people's eyes.

Emily: Can I help? I have a lot of time on my hands, and I'd like to be actively involved. Maybe I could help with the soup kitchens, or … or visit the poor wretches in gaol, or something? If that's all right with you, George?

George: Of course, my dear. Whatever makes
   you happy.

Charles Dickens: Then we will talk. There is much to
   be done. But the word is spreading, and I really
   think we can make a difference. Despite it all,
   I have great hopes for the future.

Emily: To the future, then!

   *(**Emily** raises her glass. **George** and **Charles
   Dickens** raise theirs.)*

George and Charles Dickens: The future! *(They drink)*

EPILOGUE

(The entire Cast)

*Sissy and **Charles Dickens** stand at opposite
ends of an empty stage. They speak directly to
the audience.*

Sissy: I never saw Mr. Dickens again. I wanted to tell
Alice and Ellen about meeting him, but they were
busy with the guest upstairs. I was down in the
scullery, washing dishes as usual. They wouldn't
have believed me, anyway. People like me don't
have conversations with famous writers.

Charles Dickens: She's wrong, of course. How does she
think I get all my ideas?

*(The rest of the **Cast** quietly file in as **Sissy** speaks.)*

Sissy: I've still got his hanky, mind.
I washed it and put it through the mangle. See?
(She holds it up) It's got letters embroidered on
it. I reckon they stand for his name, though I
can't be sure. I'm going to keep it always, to
remind me of him.

Charles Dickens: Good grief.

Sissy: Anyway, thanks to him, I've still got my job. The dinner went well, so I hear. The guest upstairs sent his compliments to Mrs. Fry, which put her in a good mood.

Charles Dickens: It was indeed an excellent meal. Particularly the broiled mackerel. Done to a turn.

Sissy: She's packed up the leftovers, and she says I can take them round to Ma tomorrow, so long as I'm quick. Will she be pleased to see me! The change from the sovereign will pay off the back rent owing, so that'll be one worry less. It might even stretch to a drop of fresh milk for the little 'uns.

Charles Dickens: *(Sighs)* And all for the price of a box of cigars.

Sissy: Mr. Dickens was right, of course. It is a hard world, in lots of ways. But things can only get better. Right?

The Cast: Right!

Sissy: *(To audience)* Well, it's been another long day. You can stay up if you like. I'll leave you to turn off the gas. *(Yawns)* Me, I'm going to bed.

The End

About the play

The play is designed to be read in approximately
30 minutes.

You may wish to act it out in Assembly, in modern dress.

If you put on a full-scale production with an invited
audience, you may wish to flesh the play out a little.
For example, the choir could sing a selection of Victorian
songs during scene changes. You could include an
introduction in which children explain that the play is
part of a Victorian project. They could describe some of
the things they have learned about Victorian life in order
to "set the scene".

Staging

There are six scenes in the play. If you are using a fixed
stage, it is best to keep scenery and props to a minimum.
If you have rostra blocks, you can add extra acting areas.
If you are working without a stage or blocks, simply mark
off the acting area with masking tape.

The only essential large props are a table and some chairs.
If all the scenes are to be performed in one acting area,
the same table can be used for Scene 1 (the kitchen),
Scene 2 (the nursery), Scene 3 (the morning room) and
Scene 6 (the dining room). It can be dressed up with
a tablecloth, candles, glasses, etc. for the final scene.
The table can be removed for Scenes 4 and 5
(the marketplace and the alleyway).

All the small props – trays of dishes, food, etc. – can be
brought on and off by the actors. The jar of pickled onions
could be represented by a plastic screw-top jar containing
small painted balls made up from screwed-up paper. The
costermongers can have trays displaying their wares hung

round their necks. The food can be made from papier mâché.

If you have several acting areas, you may wish to use a backcloth for each scene, but this is not really necessary. The simplest solution is to perform in front of a display of children's paintings depicting Victorian times.

Scenes 2, 3 and 5 require relatively small acting areas. Scenes 1, 4 and 6 require more space.

Costume

If you are putting on a production, you will probably want to dress your cast to some extent.

The girls will require long skirts (no ankles showing!) Crinolines (hooped petticoats) can be made from wire. Borrowed bridesmaids' dresses and plain shawls would be suitable. Mob-caps (large, soft indoor hats), bonnets and aprons are easy to construct from white crêpe paper. If possible, the costumes for the kitchen staff should match. Miss Twaite could have a lorgnette, and Mrs Garnett could be dressed in black.

The boys will need a supply of waistcoats, old and new. Charles Dickens, George Nash, the gentleman and Mr Davy will need high collars and long jackets, with top hats for the first three. Henry and Jack can be in shirtsleeves and waistcoats. The urchins, the beggarwoman, the crossing sweeper and several of the costermongers will only need rags. The other costermongers can be dressed simply: shirtsleeves for the boys and long skirts for the girls. The Nash girls should wear smocks (loose dresses), with a sailor suit for Arthur (if the actor will put up with this).

Improvisation is all! Make sure you have plenty of crêpe paper and cardboard - and find the stapler! Good luck!

HODDER WAYLAND PLAYS

If you've enjoyed *Cruel Times*, try the other titles in the series:

Humble Tom's Big Trip by Kaye Umansky

Humble Tom, a shepherd boy, leaves his country home to see the world. Will he survive the rickety roads, the city crooks and the foul-tasting pottage? This hilarious farce is set in Tudor times around King Henry's VIII's voyage to the Field of the Cloth of Gold.

Bombs and Blackberries by Julia Donaldson

Britain is at war, and the Chivers' youngest children have to leave their parents to live in the countryside. They are delighted to be brought back home when it looks as though the Germans aren't going to invade after all. But the air-raid siren goes off and this time it's frighteningly real... This dramatic and touching story is set in Manchester between 1939 and 1941.

The Head in the Sand by Julia Donaldson

Arthur Godbold digs up a bronze head from a Suffolk river. As he puzzles over it, the dramatic story of the Roman invasion of Britain unfolds in front of his very own eyes. Emperor Claudius, British Queen Boudicca, Roman soldiers and British slave girls are all involved in this fascinating and exciting story.

All these books can be purchased from your local bookseller. For more information about Hodder Wayland plays, write to:

The Sales Department, Hodder Children's Books,
A division of Hodder Headline Limited, 338 Euston Road,
London NW1 3BH